ANNE
FRANK

DiscoverRoo
An Imprint of Pop!
popbooksonline.com

Emma Bassier

abdobooks.com

Published by Pop!, a division of ABDO, PO Box 398166, Minneapolis, Minnesota 55439. Copyright © 2020 by POP, LLC. International copyrights reserved in all countries. No part of this book may be reproduced in any form without written permission from the publisher. Pop!™ is a trademark and logo of POP, LLC.

Printed in the United States of America, North Mankato, Minnesota

052019
092019

THIS BOOK CONTAINS RECYCLED MATERIALS

Cover Photo: Jewish Chronicle/Heritage Image Partnership Ltd/Alamy

Interior Photos: Jewish Chronicle/Heritage Image Partnership Ltd/Alamy, 1; akg-images/Newscom, 5; iStockphoto, 6, 9, 13, 17, 21, 22 (left), 22 (right), 23 (top), 28–29; Shutterstock Images, 7, 8, 15, 30; Album/Fine Art Images/Newscom, 11, 25 (closed diary); United Archives/IFTN/Newscom, 12–13; US National Archives and Records Administration, 14; Red Line Editorial, 19; Eva Plevier/Reuters/Newscom, 20; CBW/Alamy,

23 (bottom); Andreas Arnold/dpa/picture-alliance/Newscom, 25 (open diary), 31; Guillermo Legaria/AFP/Getty Images, 26; Ton Koene/VWPics/Newscom, 27

Editor: Brienna Rossiter
Series Designer: Sarah Taplin

Library of Congress Control Number: 2018964782

Publisher's Cataloging-in-Publication Data

Names: Bassier, Emma, author.

Title: Anne Frank / by Emma Bassier.

Description: Minneapolis, Minnesota : Pop!, 2020 | Series: Amazing young people | Includes online resources and index.

Identifiers: ISBN 9781532163647 (lib. bdg.) | ISBN 9781644940372 (pbk.) | ISBN 9781532165085 (ebook)

Subjects: LCSH: Frank, Anne, 1929-1945--Juvenile literature. | Diarists--Biography--Juvenile literature. | Jewish children in the Holocaust--Biography--Juvenile literature. | Innovators--Biography--Juvenile literature.

Classification: DDC 940.5318 [B]--dc23

WELCOME TO

DiscoverRoo!

Pop open this book and you'll find QR codes loaded with information, so you can learn even more!

Scan this code* and others like it while you read, or visit the website below to make this book pop!

popbooksonline.com/anne-frank

*Scanning QR codes requires a web-enabled smart device with a QR code reader app and a camera.

TABLE OF CONTENTS

CHAPTER 1
INSPIRING DIARY

Anne Frank was a girl who lived during World War II (1939–1945). She wrote a famous diary. She wrote it while her family was hiding from the **Nazis**.

WATCH A VIDEO HERE!

Anne Frank was a young Jewish girl.

Anne and her family were Jewish.

The Nazis hated and **persecuted** Jews.

In 1933, the Nazis took over Germany's

government. They made laws that took

away Jewish people's freedom. They also

arrested or killed many Jews.

To stay safe, some Jewish

people left Germany.

But the Nazis took

over other countries.

When that happened,

many Jewish people

went into hiding.

Deutfche! Behrt Euch! auft nicht bei Juden!

This sign tells people not to buy from stores owned by Jewish people.

Anne stuck photos to some of the diary's pages.

Anne's diary describes what life in hiding was like. It also tells her thoughts and feelings.

Anne and her family hid in the upper levels of a house. The house was behind an office building.

DID YOU KNOW? Anne was 13 years old when she started writing the diary.

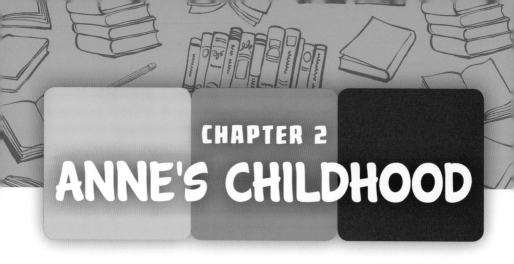

Anne Frank was born on June 12, 1929.

Otto and Edith Frank were her parents.

She had an older sister named Margot.

The Frank family lived in Germany.

When the **Nazis** took control, the

LEARN MORE
HERE!

Anne (left) and Margot stand with their mother in 1933.

Franks were not safe. They decided to

leave the country.

Anne writes at a desk.

They moved to the Netherlands
in 1933. The Franks lived in the city of
Amsterdam. Anne went to school there.
She had many friends.

DID YOU KNOW?

Anne wanted to become a writer. She wrote and edited stories.

German troops took over several countries in Europe.

But the Nazis **invaded** the

Netherlands in 1940. They made more

laws against Jews. Soon, Jews could

not go to parks or restaurants. Nazis

could take their homes or belongings.

Nazis made Jewish people wear a yellow star on their clothes. It identified them as Jewish.

Nazis even stopped Jewish children from going to school. Once again, the Franks were in danger. This time, they decided to hide.

DID YOU KNOW? The Nazis made more than 2,000 laws against Jewish people.

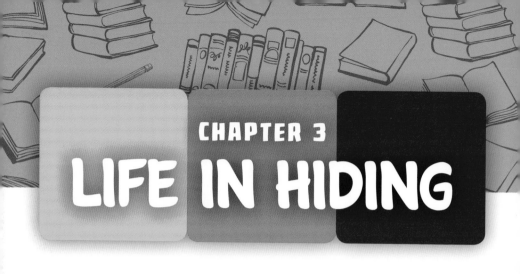

CHAPTER 3
LIFE IN HIDING

Anne's father owned a business in Amsterdam. A few small rooms were hidden above it. A secret entrance to the rooms was behind a bookshelf. In 1942, Anne's family moved into these rooms.

COMPLETE AN ACTIVITY HERE!

The Frank family hid in rooms attached to the back of this building.

Anne called the rooms the secret **annex**. She wrote about living there. Life in hiding was difficult. Four other people lived with the Franks. No one could go outside. And everyone had to stay quiet. If neighbors heard footsteps or voices, they might tell the **Nazis**. Then the annex would be discovered.

DID YOU KNOW? Miep Gies helped the Franks hide. She worked in the offices below the annex.

THE SECRET ANNEX

The secret annex was only part of the building.
Two floors existed below it. An attic was above the
fourth floor. And there were business offices in front of
the annex.

Fourth Floor of the Building

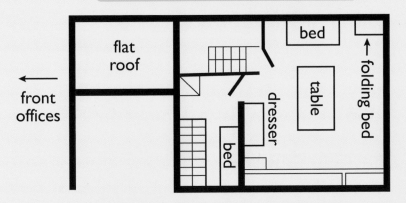

Third Floor of the Building

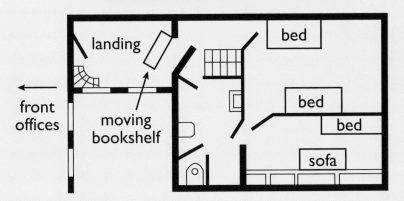

The entrance to the secret rooms was hidden by a bookshelf.

The Frank family hid for two years.

Friends brought food and news from

outside. Then, in 1944, the Nazis found

In concentration camps, hundreds of people were packed together in small buildings with wooden bunks.

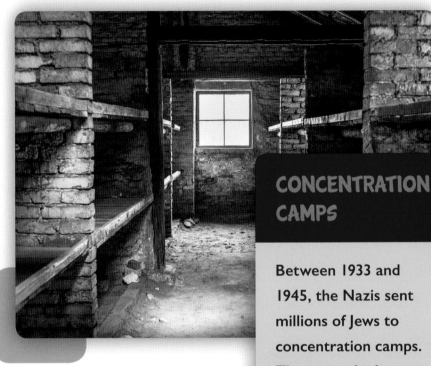

the annex. They sent Anne and the others to **concentration camps**.

CONCENTRATION CAMPS

Between 1933 and 1945, the Nazis sent millions of Jews to concentration camps. The camps had very little food or water. People lived in terrible conditions. In all, six million Jews died during this period. This event is known as the **Holocaust**.

TIMELINE

1929
Anne Frank is born on June 12 in Germany.

1933
The Franks move to the Netherlands.

1942
Anne and her family go into hiding.

1945

Anne gets sick and dies in a concentration camp called Bergen-Belsen.

1944

Nazis discover the annex.

1947

Anne's diary is published as a book called *The Diary of a Young Girl*.

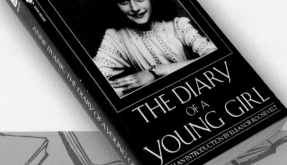

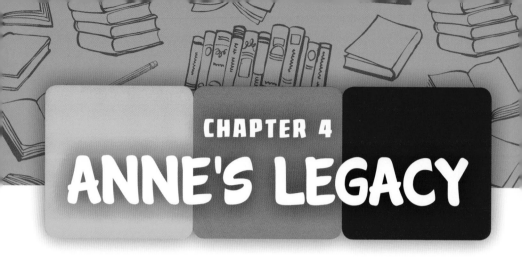

CHAPTER 4
ANNE'S LEGACY

Anne got sick in the **concentration camp**. She died in 1945. But her diary survived. A friend gave it to Anne's father after the war. Otto was the only person from the **annex** who survived.

LEARN MORE HERE!

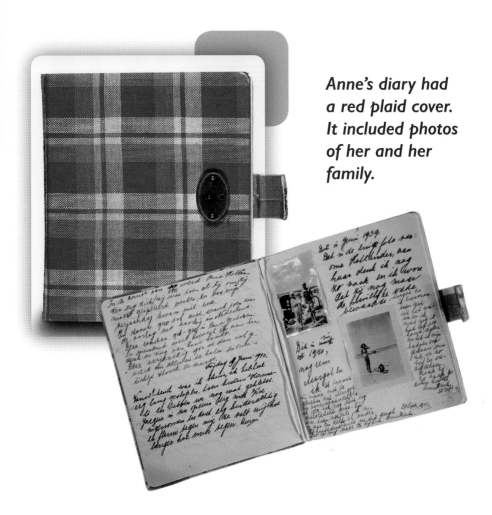

Anne's diary had a red plaid cover. It included photos of her and her family.

He put parts of the diary together to make a book. He wanted people to read about and remember Anne's life.

Girls in Colombia read about Anne Frank.

The book is called *The Diary of a Young Girl*. It was originally published in Dutch in 1947. Since then, people all over the world have read it.

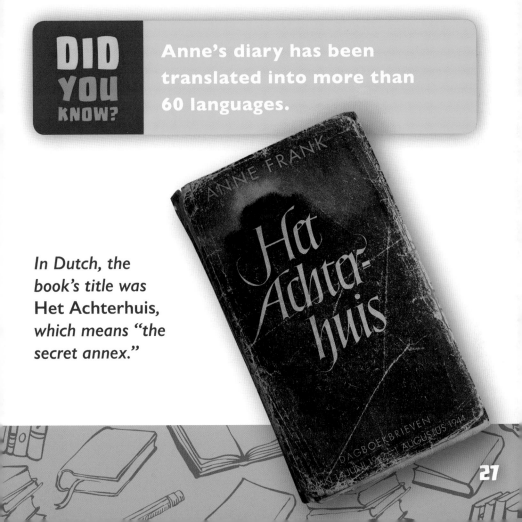

DID YOU KNOW?

Anne's diary has been translated into more than 60 languages.

In Dutch, the book's title was **Het Achterhuis,** *which means "the secret annex."*

The secret annex was hidden behind this building.

Later, the annex was turned into a

museum. The museum opened in 1960. It

is called the Anne Frank House. Visitors

can see Anne's diary on display. They can

People can visit the Anne Frank House museum to learn about Anne's life.

learn about what life was like for Jewish

people during World War II. They also

remember the **Holocaust**.

MAKING CONNECTIONS

TEXT-TO-SELF

Have you ever kept a diary or journal? What did you write about?

TEXT-TO-TEXT

Have you read another book about someone who lived during World War II? How was that person's life similar to Anne's? How was it different?

TEXT-TO-WORLD

Anne and her family were persecuted for being Jewish. What groups of people face discrimination or persecution today?

GLOSSARY

annex – a small building that is attached to a larger building.

concentration camp – a place where large numbers of people are kept as prisoners in very bad conditions, forced to do hard work, or killed.

Holocaust – the killing of six million Jewish people by the Nazis during World War II.

invade – to enter and take over an area by force.

Nazi – a member of the political group that controlled Germany during World War II.

persecute – to harm a group of people because of who they are or what they believe.

INDEX

ONLINE RESOURCES
popbooksonline.com

Scan this code* and others like it while you read, or visit the website below to make this book pop!

popbooksonline.com/anne-frank

*Scanning QR codes requires a web-enabled smart device with a QR code reader app and a camera.